HALF MOON OVER

Poems West of the Divide

By Stacey Shaw

Copyright © 2015 by Stacey Shaw. All rights reserved. No portion of this book, except for brief reviews, may be reproduced, stored in a retrieval system, or transmitted in any form or by any means – electronic, mechanical, photocopying, recording, or otherwise – without the written permission of the publisher.
For information contact Cedar & Peaches Press at cedarandpeachespress@gmail.com

Published by Cedar & Peaches Press
P.O. Box 336
The Dalles, OR 97058

Printed in the USA
Cover Photo by Stacey Shaw, all rights reserved.
Cover and Book Design by Stacey Shaw

Issued in print and electronic formats

Publisher's Cataloging in Publication
Shaw, Stacey, 1974-
Half moon over : poems west of the divide / by Stacey Shaw.
      pages cm
      LCCN 2015903749
      ISBN 978-0-9961261-0-6 (pbk.)
      ISBN 978-0-9961261-1-3 (pdf)
      1. West (U.S.)--Poetry.   I. Title.
         PS3619.H3944H35 2015   811'.6
         QBI15-600073

Dedicated to all those who know
that paying attention
is Love.

Table of Contents

Fence Line & Montana Prairie 1
Only This 2
Shall We? 3
Witness 4
Hambre del Alma / Hunger of the Soul 5
The Lifeguard 6
Beyond 7
Power: Talking to N'chi Wana 8
Precipice 9
Isla Aguada 10
White 11
Ted's Tavern 13
The Bee 14
Slot Canyon 15
Daredevil Heart 16
Forks of Salmon 17
Source and Confluence 18
Sandstone 20
Instant 21
She Who Watches 22
Excavation 25
Providers 26
Blood Moon & Turtles 27
Lucid 30

Unwoven	31
Three Shifts a Day	32
Nectar	34
Details	35
One More Day	36
Call Me Crazy	41
Reflection	42
Turns Out	44
Domestique	48
Big Night in Babb	49
Precious	51
Autumn: Washougal	52
Impatient Stories	55
Chain Gang Lunch	56
Space	58
La Unica Cosa	60

Fence Line & Montana Prairie

Horses.
There were horses,
manes wild,
storm rolling down fast
and gun metal
blue grey sky clay
so thick.
And the horses
restless with electricity
and wild with sun
from nowhere
lighting green gold grass
and a wall of steel clouds
forever long
pressing down hard.

Only This

Miracles are missed
daily.
Trampled under foot,
the impossible colors
of living things
missed,
as we keep our appointments
thinking ourselves good.

Yet, miracles do happen.
In a moment of presence
or in spite of ourselves,
we are grabbed by the chin
and made aware.

Opportunity appears
to open wide
and caution whispers
of a safer road,
closer to the one we know,
not knowing
that halfhearted love
is no longer an option.

Shall We?

First words,
then a look,
that look.
The one where your eyes
see so far into mine
seeing so deeply
into yours.
And then the words
become irrelevant,
become merely
a pleasant hum,
the strum
that begins
the fragile music of our dance.

Witness

I went to the bar tonight
to shoot pool,
hear bad tunes
and lose some agitation
amid the easy chatter
of benevolent drunks.

As usual,
when I asked to play pool
in Spanish
the young Mexican men
were eager to play
the gringa.

Tonight it was Juvenal.
He bought himself a Bud
and me a Corona,
asked me if I like to dance,
and said that his 21-year-old wife
had just kicked him out.

Then he cried,
and thanked me
for the talk.
I thanked him
for the beer.

Hambre del Alma

Tengo corazón rebelde
como un tigre corriendo
en la selva oscuro,
en la naturaleza salvaje.
Como un pájaro volando
sobre el mar
o las montañas inmensas;
como el picaflor, el colibrí
comiendo azúcar de las flores
 y el sol.

Hunger of the Soul

I have a rebellious heart
like a tiger running
in the dark jungle,
in wild nature.
Like a bird flying over the ocean
or immense mountains;
like the hummingbird,
the hummingbird
eating sugar of flowers
and the sun.

The Lifeguard

A worn string
made of stories forgotten
and a sweet dust of fondness
drifting
across an open expanse
of memory
lands in your lap.

"I wish I was there with you."

Beautiful lost man,
long ago delicate love,
an ember, seldom kissed,
who thinks of you often ~
more than you ever knew.
Or maybe you always knew.

Surfacing in a gasp,
looking for the safest way to exit
the deep end
of a wrecked pool
in a marriage ended,
or ending.

Thrashing in the water of what if,
pleading for a life ring
of attention,
pulling him gently
back to the shore
of his own Essence,
taking care
not to slip in the pool
heart first.

Beyond

Thousands of words
would fall short.
Inadequate
and barely containing
a particle of What Is.
Everything falls
into blissful silence.

Power: Talking to N'chi Wana

Beneath this reflective surface,
this subdued current,
you are a wild primal torrent.
I have heard that you killed men
in the cascades
where basalt
squeezes you in places.
The rushing soul
of a million acres
streams steadily through my body.
I know what it is to be harnessed,
to be used for the strength you possess.
Memory older than memory,
my face in your water,
your grace in my eyes,
we flow onward, through constriction,
to the wide open meandering
peaceful caress of sand.
We leave our scars to settle,
and still we flow,
carrying the tears of mountains
into the deepest embrace
of the ocean of our origin.

Precipice

Sometimes my body
just barely keeps me
from exploding
into the vast luscious space
between here
and the
perfect sunset.

Isla Aguada

Dusk in Aguada,
long and pink,
the way the sun stretched itself out
hot and lazy
over the Laguna de Terminos,
there was something about that.
We all felt it.

On the dock we sat
bathed golden in those rays.
And the Iguada Heat
shot hoops on the basketball court,
and we just fell off the dock,
floating high in the brackish water,
belly up, holding hands,
with frigate birds soaring above us.

The way the light split refracted
all orange love and crimson lust
when we squinted at the Puente de la Amistad,
there was something about that.
We all felt it.

White

In the passenger seat
of the white van,
with you in the back,
headlights off,
daring the night,
full moon
as bright as Broadway.

The squeak and crunch
of tires on packed snow,
Silver diamonds of moonlight;
sparkling for endless miles.
A thrill right there,
seeing such
hushed magic.

But then,
ghost horses.
White
on white.

Some ominous
and shimmering mirage
slowing time
to one small eternity.

Shadows racing across
that pristine pale sea.
The beat of frenzied hooves,
galloping from nowhere,
straight at us.

Wild eyes reflecting light,
bracing for impact,
as each stallion and mare
peeled off left,
right,
left,
at the last possible second.

Brushing the grill,
the sound of wild chaos
manes slapping frigid metal,
a split herd engulfing us
in billows of hot breath
and galloping on.

And suddenly,

silence

slammed so hard
into our racing hearts.

Ted's Tavern

One drunk biker
got kicked out
of a little hole in the wall bar.
He was looking for a fight.

Said he'd be back
to kick some ass,
and he was,
with the rumble of twenty hogs.

A herd of bikers
on a revenge mission,
greeted at the door
by my dad
holding a Colt Peacemaker,
and these words,

"You can come on in,
but the first six of you
aren't gonna make it."

Maybe that line was his,
maybe not,
but it worked.
They all left
and no asses were kicked.

The Bee

A bee hovers by my foot
wondering if my crimson toenails
are some strange flowers.

Smelling my scent with no hint of fear,
darting sideways and hovering still.

Slot Canyon

I have the dreams of your kind.
I have coyote's raucous screaming
and the glow of moonlight.
I have the early freeze
and the long drought.
I have the languages
that you've never heard.
I'm in cahoots with Old Crow
and the green streak
of a comet's tail.

Daredevil Heart

Others ease
into these chilly waters,
dip in a little toe
and pull back quickly,
before daring to slip back in,
only to the ankles.

But me, I alley-oop.
I swan dive… no,
cannonball.
No matter how dim
and deep the abyss,
I'll shatter through the ice
just to feel the sensation
of that cool water
on my warm skin.

Even for a second,
just to know,
how cold?
How deep?
How deliciously dark
is this pool?

Forks of Salmon

A sticky mist clings
to wet madrones,
clings
to my body.
Red curls of papery skin
now spread out
to cover smooth milky trunks.
Water drips loosely
through a green sea of leaves
as the river seduces the hillsides
with silver billows of steam.

Source and Confluence

I do love you
all the way back
to your Source,
someplace imagined
up north
where I could step
across your beginnings.

I have pictured it
while staring
at the complicated swirls
of lichen greens
and deep clay browns
where the Washougal falls into you.

The sacred confluence of water,
sacred,
even as these rivers flow
through metal
around pilings
over tires.

I know that my blood
has been carried
through this mixing place
from where I gashed my knees
and sliced my hands
swimming far upstream.

I know that this is the place
where salmon get the signal,
pick up the scent,
know to veer left
flashing their silver sides,
steady in their bearing.

I know that this place
whispered to me
to love a river
a person
an experience
a life
from confluence
to the Source.

Sandstone

I can tell you of heat,
of the red ocher
and the salmon
pink and black
of cliffs,
and a crow
riding thermal air
rising toward the sun,
and rustles
of dry leaves
cracked soles
lizard feet.

Instant

The sun bore down
hot
just moments ago it seems,
now clouds.
A white line
slices clean
through a silver curtain.

She Who Watches

My grandfather
and great-uncle
took your salmon
from the thunderous churning
of Celilo
with pitchforks.

My great-grandmother
picnicked on your islands,
crumbling smoked sturgeon
on crackers
while her brother steamed past sandbars
on the Bailey Gatzert.

They all enjoyed you.
They all used you,
and they had their children
while you watched nearby.

My father,
the young Coast Guard captain,
piloting past The Dalles,
through the tight channel
before the dam,
daydreaming
of the last fish wheel
working the river
years before.

Stationed in Pasco,
and down at Ilwaco,
pulling the capsized
from the frigid fate
you tossed them
while crossing your bar,
where you slam into the Pacific
like an angry lover.

My father, like his father,
worked in a paper mill
on your shore
using your water
to cool machines
and always fishing.

I grew up with you giving.
We watched each other.
In a boat below Bonneville,
our hearts hurt together.
Your currents asked me questions
I could not answer
while the old fishing platforms
told me stories about your true soul.

I tried to leave,
to turn away
but I saw you anyway,
in Mexico, on television,
flowing past in Spanish.

El Río Columbia
tiene mucha contaminación
y esta lo mas en peligro
en los Estados Unidos.

There were dreams,
meanderings,
and stories
that wove a heartstring here.
I knew I'd return,
on some level, to you.

Primordial matriarch,
beloved friend,
shadow of your former Self,
greater than the sum of your basalt chunks,
survivor of industrial assault,
and still,
the most glorious thing I know.

Let me tell you
my ancestors have regrets.

Excavation

Little rivers
in deep tracks
of Earth movers,
little rivers
of brown
water and oil
in what was
a meadow.

Providers

With rough hands
and jaws set,
hauling up the net
hand over hand,
blood smears the ropes
as diamonds of sun
glint off the frenzied water.
They squint, are silent, taste salt.
Salmon tails slap the deck
and gills heave
in desperate spasm.
Gulls fix intense yellow-lined eyes
on the hands
of these well-intentioned men.

Blood Moon & Turtles

The orange glow
of oil rigs
low on the horizon
bringing the blood moon
to light the beach.

Jaime had already left
on the other moto.
I stood watch
with Ricardo,
one green turtle
and ten thousand flies.

Pulling black pantyhose
over my face,
lying in the sand
collecting eggs and sleeping
until the tide went out again
just before dawn.

They say Concho's grandpa,
back when he was mayor,
jailed a statue.
Threw it in solitary.

For years it sat in a cell alone
for killing a man
by tipping off a high pedestal
in the church courtyard
dropping onto the skull
of a man as he lay napping;
an out-of-towner, from the city.

The bust of Benito Juarez
charged with manslaughter.

Some nights we go to war.
The locals still love
their turtle soup and eggs
and we have some reckless chase
through sea grape and plastic bags,
the ever present scent of grass fire
in the air.

They on foot
butchering the turtle.
Maybe two, maybe ten,
hacking off flippers on the run.
We can hear their footfall
and hushed cries
just beyond
the beam of our headlight.

Following fresh
hot blood trails in the sand,
and I know
we could be killed right here.
And I know it would be
some gruesome death.
But in this moment,
this moment is all there is.
And without a thought this seems
as good a moment to die
as any other.

Some nights we sing
as earnestly as we can,
as though
for the purest love of one another.

You sing every song you know
in English
which is only two Beatles
and one Frank Sinatra.

I did it my way.

And some mornings
when we finish
just after daybreak
we go to the 24/7
truck stop taco joint
by the bridge.
And you bring up the time
I tried to tell you to buy
chicken breasts for dinner,
"chichis de pollo"

because, really,
who knows the word pechuga
until you have to use it?

And tears ran down your face
as you drew a buxom chicken
wearing a bra
and taped it to the fridge.

"Hey, why don't you order a chicken tit taco?"

you say and fall out of your chair
laughing
as I eye the menu and
say good morning to the cook.

Lucid

Poetry comes in bed,
revealing
and retreating,
a tease.

In the hours when
sleep would be better,
a crystalline string
of a spider web
floats in the air,
in the periphery
in a squint
reflecting sunlight.

When I go to look for it
it is nowhere.

We drift
into grief
into sleep
into death
and poetry comes to dance
in our bed
and sometimes never waltzes
with waking,
but only holds us close
at the wake.

Unwoven

Take it.
Your voodoo,
your spells,
a drapery of words
threaded and sewn
with a needle sharp tongue
piercing the hopeful clothing
of so many generations.
For how long?
For only this long.
The spool is bare.
So go ahead,
take it.
I will go naked.

Three Shifts a Day

I remember the guy
who patiently told me
to practice
staying inside the lines,
leaning over my book.

He sat on my right
at the end of the bar.
His brown hair hanging,
my crayon purple,
his breath sweet
with decay and cheap beer.

I can't remember the bartender,
but I remember pickled eggs in a jar,
and my Shirley Temple,
the taste of a dyed red cherry,
the black vinyl topped stools.
And his name was Dee,
pretty sure, not Virgil
or Fred.

The walk-in, a frigid blast,
sticky white tile floor,
the scent of stale booze.
Playboy and Playgirl centerfolds
wallpaper the bathrooms,
jukebox in the corner,
pay phone by the thick wood door
smears of black stains
on the handle side
from greasy hands
stumbling out.

A long lamp hanging low
over the pool table,
Crumb's 'Stoned Agin' poster
on the wall.
All more interesting
than those long hours
sitting out in the car.

Happy enough to be coloring
with one of the regulars,
in the corner bar by the mill,
7-up, grenadine and one cherry.

Nectar

I don't know how it happens.
I only know that
there is something sweet
deep down
just below the surface.
How is it that I never sensed it
all those years before?
Because from the day
I finally noticed
it is the only thing
I would give anything
to taste.

Details

Yesterday I saw your toes,
grotesque sausages,
lovely nubs,
tan or dirty,
they shocked me
in their utterly
perfect
imperfection.

One More Day

Stuck with the taffy makers
slapping and stretching
sugar cane boiled in water
from sticky lumps
on wooden pegs,
into long silky ropes.

In a fine little place
with a local family,
you got cabin fever,
needed to bolt.
"Where?"
"Anywhere."

But there were riots
over gas prices
and mountains of tires.
Fires
burning in the streets,
tear gas and tanks
rolling on school kids in Quito.

An election year to boot,
harassing gringos
on every bus out of town
just to make a point of it.
I wasn't going anywhere today,
and man,
did that piss you off.

But we were safer here
than on the ferrocarril
to murder central,
on the Columbian border.

Where people disappear
every damn day
like fog in the sun,
just evaporated.

The rickety one track,
two car train
out to the coast from Ibarra
swarmed right on the platform,
a desperate mob
robbed and pushed us
to the back of the car.

Broke down suddenly
in a long dark tunnel
surrounded by those
five guys
who'd already threatened us
openly
for hours on end.

Pitch black,
split second,
threw the window down
tossed out my pack
& jumped
landing ankle deep
in gasoline.

"Throw me your pack and jump",
I yelled up.
Now.
Right now.
No questions and
thank God
you had faith,
and hiked out to the light.

Safer than riding
on top of the train
because inside we were prey,
cornered on the roof
by a huge guy asking his gang
for just one reason
why he shouldn't kill
two white whores,
tossing our bodies from the top
before the next stop.

Staring us down
hundreds of miles of threats
rolling off his tongue
like water
like blood
like disappearing fog,
just evaporating.

Safer than walking
home in the city
hearing the downshift
behind us
seeing the guy pull up
beside me
pants down, dick in hand,
shouting, "get in the car."

Safer than holding on
to thin worn ropes
digging into our palms
with one strapped down pig
on top of that bus
(on top of all the damned buses)
careening around a blind corner

brakes slammed
just inches from a head on
on a nearly washed out
mountainside road
in the middle of nowhere
time and again,
and again.

No, we're in a fine place tonight.
This internal courtyard,
locked gates on the street side,
broken glass tops the walls.

Let the tires burn out there.
Let that violence be.
Let the men want us
and the women spite us
and most just hate us.

Out there, where our skin
and the color of our eyes
look like oppression
and colonization
and cultural genocide,
like death.

Out there,
where we could be killed
tonight
for looking like the killers
of centuries.

We're in a fine place
to eat fried plantains, again,
with rice and chicken, again.
Listen to the pouring rain,
read another Márquez
and wonder what the hell
we've chosen to see,
again.

Call Me Crazy

I talk to people
that I wish
were here.

Reflection

You only want to know me
just enough to judge me,
only enough
to find the words
to craft an effective arrow
and locate the softest spot
to take aim.

You only want to know
enough
to find a fatal flaw
enough
to find the nails
to hang me on
to wield control
in the name of help.

Help,
to be someone else,
but not just anyone,
only to be like you,
(because I need to be fixed
don't cha know).

Only enough
to aim enough shame
to keep me in line,
like the shame
that kept you in line
and your folks
and theirs.

Just enough
to keep me
from telling you the truth
about yourself
without a word,
just by Being;
unashamed
and proud.

Even if
I only dare speak it
by my dignity,
or my clarity,
or with one simple question.

Even if in all that Beauty
I see in you
I will not look away
or choke on my own tongue
because I don't bite it,
you only see in horror
the clear mirror
you try to shatter,
for reflecting
what you have spent a lifetime
trying not to see.

Enough.

Turns Out

"It's where they took my guts out",
my brother said flippantly
brushing his teeth,
shirtless.

Sitting on the kitchen counter
of the cabin
we called a house.
Fifteen years between us,
I'd asked about his scar.

The huge one,
a wide purple slash
across his side,
his belly,
asked in the raw
confronting way
that only small children do.

Guts.

The only guts I knew were fish guts.

The ones my dad talked about
down at the ponds
of trout, salmon, sturgeon,
as he plunged a filet knife
into those soft white bellies,
scales on his knuckles
instructing me
on the removal of guts.

And so I imagined
that my brother
had been full
of pink salty fish eggs.

We visited him in the hospital
like always.
Long white tile hallways,
secrets held behind
swinging double doors.
Sitting.
      Waiting.

But this time we all went in
and he was lying on the bed
with a big square hole
cut into his body,
just empty to the spine,
just hollow.

A cavity all cleaned out
and we were in good spirits,
stood around talking
and I looked to the faces
of the adults
to see if I should be horrified;
but they weren't
and so I wasn't.

I was nineteen when
I fully realized
that was just a dream
when I knew
that there was nothing at all
about that image
that held any truth.

Turns out
it was his spleen,
those guts.
Turns out
when he was six
they didn't know much
about kidney disease.
He'd undergo procedures
experimental,
unnecessary.

He wasn't supposed to live
to be twelve,
two failed transplants
by eighteen,
no kidneys at all until death,
at nearly fifty,
some kind of record
no one wants to hold.

When they cut off part of a toe
he was done with it all,
no more needles
not another machine,
refused his dialysis,
and let everyone know,
it's time.

To let go into
that unbelievable pain
that was always his burden to feel,
laying it all down,
folding his hand
at long last.

Turns out
he was one tough
son of a bitch.
But then again,
he had to be.

Guts.

Domestique

The flowers on our table have begun to wilt
reminding me of my cage.

The beauty of something wild always fades
in a lovely glass jar.

Big Night in Babb

We landed
beside the cows
and molehills as big as our tires.
A grassy field
with a bleached out
tattered windsock.
Everyone said,
"You can't fly a plane
in Glacier National Park",
but you'd studied your airspace,
and so we did.

Low in the passes
and over knife edge ridges,
downdrafts from hell,
thousand foot elevators be damned.
Just hold on and hold your breath kid.

Hitchhiking to the nearest bar,
drinking shit beer,
with a toothbrush in my shirt pocket,
cringing at your jokes
that I won't repeat even now.
Keeping a wary eye on the locals
for keeping their wary eyes on us,
waiting 'til my friend
(grill cook at the diner)
got off work.

You slept on her couch that night
in your tighty whities
while we laughed until we cried,
splitting our sides.
The plane tied down
in that lonely field 'til morning.

Until we'd had our bacon
and our coffee black,
and who knows
which way the wind was blowing
or what the cows were thinking.

Precious

Who makes you laugh
more than anyone ever has?
What have you gained,
labored to acquire,
now under lock and key
that you would not give away
eagerly
in your final illness?

Grateful for each breath
in your beautiful
wrinkled temple,
the priceless medicine will be this:

to hear the voice
and see the face
of the One
who conjures streams of sacred tears
bursting from your eyes
howling to the skies
falling on one another in
belly aching
pants pissing
gut churning
laughter.

Autumn: Washougal

One morning each year
the puddles were finally frozen
on the long dawn walk
to the bus stop.

Stepping through each one,
hearing thick white ice creak,
watching trapped air moving beneath,
until the exquisite shatter
was pure joy.

The first hard freeze
in the late fall
when the filberts
had already fallen,
the swarms of summer mayflies
long forgotten.

Walking the quarter mile
to gram & gramps
because I already hated
the sound of football
and the lazy game day.

Going out to the barn
to daydream and pedal
on the homemade grinding wheel,
like some primitive bike
leading a peloton of pioneers,
imagining the hot sparks flying
and the gentle scrape
of metal blades on the thick stone.

Cutting apples for cider,
Paul on his stool fast as can be
with his Old Timer pocket knife.

The soothing hollow thump
of half apples into buckets,
pumping water from the well,
filling jugs,
feeding the barn cats.

My favorite old cow,
her thick black neck
slid though the slots,
waiting for the hay,
her hot breath hitting my face
as I spread it in the trough.

The fall hunting, a drudgery
in the truck crawling along
endless and slow
on every logging road
in the county and out,
scared shitless each time
we turned around,
every spot too narrow,
every cliff too steep.

Plywood on the kitchen table
hand sharpening worn old knives
on wet round palm stones.
Butchering: a ritual
of white paper, shiny on one side,
the coolers,
the carcass,
red and smooth,
muscle on bone,
sinew and fascia.

The cutting, the slicing,
wrapping slabs of bloody meat,
taped and labeled,
until a whole animal
was stacked neatly in the freezer.
You never asked if you could stop.
It was done when it was done,

when it was done.

Impatient Stories

Stories exist
that are begging to be told.
Stories!
Listen up!
No begging!
I am writing as fast as I can.
You need to be patient
and wait your turn.

Chain Gang Lunch

Over fifty days of rain
in a row.
Nothing new,
but a flood none the less.
Manhole covers blowing off
at the bottom of Harrison
and Capitol Lake,
water jumping over asphalt
to the Sound.

Salmon swimming across
roads in Shelton
blocking traffic,
and there we were
in our musty kitchen,
pasty white like some
damp cave dwelling moles.

On the campus station
came a plea between songs
to help set sandbags
and keep the Nisqually from
flooding the reservation school.
And what better did I have to do?
Stare at the downpour
and make more oatmeal?

The only volunteer,
the lone person
arriving to work for free,
soaked to the bone,
just me and the convicts.
Murderers, arsonists, rapists
and me.

And the National Guard,
or was it the Army
from Fort Lewis?
Soldiers with machine guns
and the inmates working
in their prisoner orange;
some in shackles.

Throwing bags to one another,
piling them up against the water.
Jokes flying,
lunch in the cafeteria,
shuffling in their jumpsuits,
guards and guns at every door.

Small talk going down the line,
our trays piled high
with canned corn and mashed potatoes.
They were so confused
about why the hell
I was with them
(and we had that in common).

But I could see their joy
just to talk to someone from
the outside;
just to be seen,
to have something there besides
the rain and chains,
guns and labor
and regrets much heavier than stone;
eating with such a strange girl
on such a rainy day.

Space

Falling forward
was always such a siren song,
with my tiny feet hanging over
that high cliff above the river.
The place I went a thousand times,
a sheer rock wall
a hundred feet down.
The sensation?
Drunk with longing,
some sort of strange rapture,
my heart had its desire,
not the impact,
not the falling,
just the merging into space.

Space.

Imagining that it could be
floating
or flying,
feeling the curse of gravity,
and the longing for
the release of
a vast light spirit from
a dense heavy body.

And then there was
the bigger cliff,
the longer drop,
and me, on my tree.

Climbing slowly down
below the steep edge
and sliding far out
onto the trunk grown sideways
in that rock wall
just to feel nothing below
and so far down,
to see my own feet
dangling in space
and wonder
what is the opposite of vertigo?

Space.

"Suicidal ideation"
my friend would
say most surely and
in his cocky way
when we watched the sunset once
on the top of a canyon ridge
and I asked him if
he ever just wanted
to dissolve
into that vast infinite Beauty

or
  fall
    out
      into
        all
          that
            space.

La Unica Cosa

The bus pulled away
just as we all realized
the young man stepping off
had everything.

My money,
my identity,
a practiced slight of hand
and he got it all.

Everyone on that bus
was appalled and angry.
They yelled
while I went blank,
my mind coming
to one silent place.

And then a huge man
came to my seat.
Standing in the aisle
he said,
"Don't worry.
You are family now.
You will come to my home."

And so I did.

Hojancha,
a man named after his place.

In that small home
I was given a smaller room
with a bare hanging light bulb,
and we ate rice with beans
and Lizano sauce
three times a day.

He argued with the embassy,
gave me keys
to a tiny apartment
in San Jose,
sent his son to travel
to the city with me,
and he brought me food
as I stood in line all day.

The whole family joined me
in that tiny apartment.
They killed a chicken
and packed the meat
so that I'd have
it to eat in the airport,
a gesture
that cracked open my heart.

And each time I tried to thank him
the only thing
Hojancha said
over and over
and over again
was this:
En la vida, la unica cosa es amigos.

In life, the only thing is friends.

www.ingramcontent.com/pod-product-compliance
Lightning Source LLC
Chambersburg PA
CBHW020959090426
42736CB00010B/1386